MW01200210

Hold Like Owls

Hold Like Owls

Julia Koets
Foreword by Nikky Finney

THE UNIVERSITY OF SOUTH CAROLINA PRESS

*Published in Cooperation with the South Carolina Poetry Initiative,
University of South Carolina*

Published by the University of South Carolina Press
Columbia, South Carolina 29208

www.sc.edu/uscpress

Manufactured in the United States of America

21 20 19 18 17 16 15 14 13 12   10 9 8 7 6 5 4 3 2 1

Library of Congress Cataloging-in-Publication Data

Koets, Julia.
  Hold like owls : poems / Julia Koets ; foreword by Nikky Finney.
    p. cm.
  "Published in Cooperation with the South Carolina Poetry Initiative,
  University of South Carolina."
  ISBN 978-1-61117-084-9 (pbk : alk. paper)
  I. Title.
  PS3611.O3647H65 2012
  811'.6—dc23

                                                    2011052080

The South Carolina Poetry Book prize is an annual prize given to the winning manuscript of a contest organized and sponsored by the South Carolina Poetry Initiative. The winning title is published by the University of South Carolina Press in cooperation with the South Carolina Poetry Initiative.

Contents

IV

Foreword

The role of the poet is not just to tell but to imagine—then illumine. The role of the poet is not just to bear witness—never to preach—but make us see, remember, recall, reach, open up both doors of the universe.

The title, and first image, owls, this ancient holy bird of the world, this great symbol of knowledge and of warning, holds sway throughout this powerful first collection.

Then the poet jumps us to moths and paper birds, but do not worry, there is still connection and wonder, and the mother image will return to make us turn our heads, all the way around in a revolution of mindfulness, without consideration of rules and limitations, that usually come along with necks.

> Moths must tire of sleeping near the ceiling.
> All that waiting for their wings to match
> color that changes where wall folds to eave.
> ("Paper Birds")

And our flight through this landscape of winged things continues:

> This afternoon I found her at the table, asleep
> among paper, delicate as dreams, elaborate
> birds made of folding, made for our ceiling.
> ("Paper Birds")

This is a graceful book of winged things. A quick glance at the titles that await in the table of contents draws the reader in right from the first:

"Fruit in Bed"
"Wide-Eyed and Song"
"A History of Hair"
"Apples and Aristophenes"
"Shrug of Broken Egg, Frozen Shell"

The dream-state is here, the surreal too. The mind of the poet is eccentric, spilling, surprising our thoughts, so gifted and so highly imaginative.

> "She has a hard time with libraries, the giving back, she said."
> ("Shrug of Broken Egg, Frozen Shell")

Composed and crafted in a myriad of forms, four-line indented stanzas or breezy couplets, stanzas composed in 4–6–4, the rhyme is almost always free, but the rhythm is controlled and the thinking—boundless:

> "I hear books melt in Phoenix if you leave them too long."
> ("Gift to a Girl in Phoenix")

The job of the poet is to slow us down, remind us of what could be? Yes.

> The night's thatched with black
> > and grown wild and secret with a floor
>
> of her shirts.
> > ("Above the Floors")

This is a poet with long extensive poetic legs. She uses them to jump, leap, land. Wherever she steadies herself in this book is indeed her country.

"I want you loud and kissing me tonight on a street we knew
    last year,"

("Wide-Eyed and Song")

There is the straight narrative, and there is the under-humming
voice, the winding looping one—the one that moves and sweeps
throughout the narrative with magic and always new possibility.

The new poetry of America, of the twenty-first century, is not
about new subjects, but it is about new ways of making the old
subjects occupy new strata. How Julia Koets thinks, then com-
poses, is both halves of that contemporary magic. She has a pen-
chant for surprising metaphor. She possesses a personal delight
for the highest flying verbs and their alluring descriptors.

> Small bundle swaddled against your back
> he hasn't learned why we are afraid, why
> lonesome, here, can be worse than dying.
>
> I tell him of cities left in sand; his fist, tight
> around my finger, holding what we have of day.
>
> ("Gentle Corners of the Night")

or

> She sells jars of pickled okra, green
> and yellow beans, and watermelon rinds.
> Her hands, accustomed to pots of vinegar
> and garlic, are pruned like a child's toes
> too long in a warm bath.
>
> ("Parking Lot Market")

There is always connection in the thinking and in the crafting
of the poem. Commas and enjambed lines mark the breathless
white space.

These are quiet poems. These are poems that come from a careful, artful noticing, poems that save something that needs to be saved. These are poems that shape-shift and then tumble off into the space of our hearts to live long after the lips and eyes first closed around them.

The different form of each poem reflects the different spirit of the other. Julia Koets is a poet who believes in staying true to what the spirit of the poem has revealed. These are *poems* that articulate the human's heart longing to understand what the head has a hard time wrapping itself around.

> Her cage was the one at the top of the hill: pool
> dirty with upcountry clay, two tires scattered
> in dust . . .
>
> Thick-skinned and dry, beast which Aristotle wrote
> passeth all others in wit and mind, accompanied
> the lonely river my grandmother waked
> with my brother and me some Saturdays.
> ("Joy, the Elephant, Greenville Zoo, 1990")

Nikky Finney

Acknowledgments

Grateful acknowledgment is made to the editors of the following publications in which these poems first appeared:

Indiana Review: "Shrug of Broken Egg, Frozen Shell"
Los Angeles Review: "Paper Birds"
undefined Magazine: "For Julia in Little Armenia"
Euphony: "Gentle Corners of the Night"
Cutthroat, a Journal of the Arts: "Fallen"

I would like to thank Scott Gould and Fred Dings, my M.F.A. workshops at the University of South Carolina, and the Prague Summer Program. Special thanks are owed to Susan Brownlee, Robin Caine, Amy Wilson-Stayton, Julia Callander, Adriana Ruvalcaba, Robin Phillips, Anne Fishwick, Lindsay Dukes, Darien Cavanaugh, Jonathan Maricle, Rachel Malis, and Lindsey Kurz for reading these poems in all stages of completeness. I am also grateful to Nikky Finney for her selection of this book. Thanks are owed to Kwame Dawes and Charlene Spearen for all they do and have done for the South Carolina Poetry Initiative.

Special thanks go to Kerri Kiernan, whose art I have on my walls at home, for the cover image for this book.

I am grateful to my parents and my brother for always reading my poems.

I

Paper Birds

Moths must tire of sleeping near the ceiling.
All that waiting for their wings to match
color that changes where wall folds to eave.

This afternoon I found her at the table, asleep
amongst paper, delicate as dreams, elaborate
birds made of folding, made for our ceiling.

I try unfolding one, tail and beak of pleats,
green and yellow flowers on a patch
of wing. No cuts or glue to hold to evening,

to have them flying from fishing line. Geese,
swans, a hummingbird. Window unlatched,
and wind wakes their sleeping from the ceiling.

Song of paper rustling; song of crease
and bend; song of watching
color that changes where wall folds to eave.

We fall asleep like this, a counting sheep,
a listening for paper birds, a grasping
for sounds that sleep near the ceiling,
in colors that change where wall folds to eave.

Woman Drawn with Stars

Mucha painted a woman with red flowers
about her head to match her lips and the beads

down her neck. To rest your cheek against
your palm is to wonder where planes go

when extinct. They rust in the sky. They let
their parts fall back to Earth. There are so many
stars I cannot connect. Sink deeper, painted

woman, into this chair of cloth and wine
until the pattern of folds
down your robe makes sense.

Shrug of Broken Egg, Frozen Shell

She has a hard time with libraries. The giving
back, she said. On a Tuesday night bits of things
leftover went underwater when she made ice cubes
with roadside peanut shells, dried sand crabs, stones

she picked up somewhere, rind of lemon, orange,
apple skin. And after they all turned to ice, she hung
them from porch banister and patio chair with string.
To hear the sounds they made dropping: thud of thawed

lemon, tinker of her last apartment key, all the sudden
letting go. Chicken bone barely there, a wet match
left beside the sink. It's raining on her porch, giving
the night a creek to listen for, a boat to fill up.

She puts a plastic Buddha in a jar with buttons
and yarn. Tops the glass with water, waits for him
to freeze. A backwards baking moves her about
the kitchen with bean snaps in a water vase, and
when the freezer gets too full and one not-yet-frozen

breaks with fluted wine glass on the tile, she is only
disappointed for sound come too early. Strange
ceremony—waiting for sound to hit the floor.

Fruit in Bed

We make ink of cherries, dark
on our fingers, and a cloak
of a bed. Numbers are missing,

or white with the sheets,
but arms find each other
in turning past the hours. Or

in a park all grass
and fountain, your shirt
rolled to pillow our heads.
Fruit rests longer
from many stems.

White on the Fence

Some loves are hidden at night, when time
       cannot be told on the face of a shadow
clock statued in the yard. Moonflowers open
white on the fence, and moths try to make sense
       of porch lights with their wings.

To love in the shadows is to know
       even your bones:
curve of your clavicle, hold of your hip; we know
each other uncovered in dark, in bumping against the edge
       of the kitchen table on the way to the sink
for a glass of water to cool our mouths.

Apples and Aristophanes

*"After the division the two parts of man, each desiring his other
half, came together, and throwing their arms about one another,
entwined in mutual embraces, longing to grow into one . . ."*

Aristophanes, Plato's "Symposium"

It is not always the best advice to love a man
for who he is. Unless his arms are a portion
of yourself. Phaedrus said love is a mighty god,
a thing even those who worship cannot explain.

You will know love as you know your own hands,
places my fingers trace, the birthmark on your knee
you tell me stories of, mapping your scars like lands
made both old and new by the scraping sea.

It is the right kind of madness to see the beauty of apples
cut in half. Fruit of one mind, split and bearing two faces.
How ancient is this desire for one another, a grappling
more precious than color, the flesh, or a place.

Blue Hour

The owls are about to leave, holding
fast to branches of magnolia. Grapefruit knives
must have another name, you ask the morning.

Teeth that curve easily with rind, corner
the edge, the divides. Taking its time
with your hands, their sleepy hold.

I hear a plane before I see it, old
sound through the sky, a question I'd like
to answer, to spend the blue before morning

with sounds that come first: the fold
of certain consonants, first bite
of a word. Opening its mouth, dawn holds

us for an hour, lets the owls learn more
about the tree, the distance between mice
and branch. The kitchen window lets morning

in your hair, has us eating toast, sorting
coffee grains. Barefoot, with your knee beside
your chest, you sit at the table, holding
a knife, whose name you ask the morning.

The Sweet of Strawberries

What are we doing with all this writing,
all that's been said four hundred times over?
Light comes through so many windows.

There's a certain slant of sun
leaving the shadows of leaves
on the wall next to my bed.

To write in the morning
is to remember our dreams,

to give the sound of our waking
a place to settle down

next to a bowl of strawberries,
cut and sweet.

When loss leans like a broken tree

after Mary Oliver

two turtles stretch out their feet and sun. The lake
        ripples to make room for its leaves, still

green after leaning. Here, turtles find a place
        to steady their shells and stick out their heads

for something other than food. Their eyes are closed
        as I watch from the edge where the roots of what's fallen

still hold on.

Gift to a Girl in Phoenix

She'd never seen roly-polies, never heard
        their names. Layers that allow them to fold
into themselves. Our first date was accidental,

which doesn't make sense if you've never been
        without a certain kind of assumption: an ease
of boy meets girl. I searched for roly-polies
        as a child under bricks not cemented down

to the dirt. Blocks unmortared for them
        to crawl under and for me to uncover.
Palms still until she uncurled her armor
        that was her body, let her tiny legs try

out my arms. I know to leave holes
        in a cardboard top if I'm cruel enough to keep her,
pray she comes out of herself, unfolds long,
        a gray inch in my hand.

I hear books melt in Phoenix if you leave them
        too long. A tired heat comes up with the sun
a kind of hot that sits you down too long
        inside. Women spin paper, grow oranges

that split open before they're ripe to eat.
      Afraid she might be dead before mail arrives
at your door five hours away by car,
      I question this present, this holding on

to my memory of something you told me
      you'd never heard of before. Would she
die with her arms wrapped around her knees
      if she had them? Or could she make it to unfold

in your hand? Even the letters must be hot
      where you're living. Unbearable to hold just yet.

Above the Floor

The night's thatched with black,
      grown wild and secret with a floor

of her shirts. An Oxford here,
      unpaired socks, a tank-topped chair,

I look up to the ceiling, where the stitching's worn
      thin, to find glowing

plastic stars coming almost through. Tangle
      of hair, nest of sheets, small green lights

fall asleep sometime after we forget,
      still awake, that they were over us at all.

Bruise

I often drove over a hill with a girl
　　　where our town turned
into another, past scattered tractor parts,
　　　house hollowed out, a wandering dog,
a chiropractor sign made from real back bones.

Parked by a strip mall, her voice fit inside
　　　a chestnut shell. She told me she never wanted
to talk in a parking lot.
　　　She would sit in a house where walls
could hear us
　　　figuring it out in the small
of the South's back. We were too afraid
to kiss a woman, then,
until it bruised, wore us
down to girls
we no longer recognized.

Wanderings

Magnolias make a mess of the stars
in a night made of crows. Birds
look to the sky to tell themselves how

they were born; how they came
to hop on two feet and fly with centuries
sounding in their wings. Crows perch

on our roof and look in our window panes,
having followed our talking out of the trees.

Wide-Eyed and Song

You have the length of a dragonfly,
come and go from six directions. Land
behind a woman's ear; make it quite

possible to hold a single reed of grass; kite
just above the ponds I carry in my hand.
You have the length of a dragonfly,

and memory gets longer out of sight,
all abdomen and thorax, and wings can
grow under water until it's quite

certain that you're more bird, wide-eyed
and song. Your laugh cannot
be quiet, grows the length of a dragonfly.

I want you loud and kissing me tonight
on a street we knew last year. Sand
knows how to go back until July's quite

hot and the linden tree is beside
itself with blooms. Memory gets longer and
has the humming length of a dragonfly,
blue when you catch it by the tail, not quite.

II

Gentle Corners of the Night

Small bundle swaddled against your back,
he hasn't learned why we are afraid, why
lonesome, here, can be worse than dying.

For months without knowing, he was kept safe
inside another life, held gentle into the night.
One thing your father still does like a child
is fly. But he is aware of the strings, wind aging

under the kite. You cannot unlearn why
we are afraid, but dream so often in the dark.
All the stories children hear fill the places
we'll never see: gentle corners of the night.

I tell him of cities left in sand; his fist, tight
around my finger, holding what we have of day.
He has not yet learned why we are afraid,
why strings can never keep things safe.

About Boats

A tin boat rubs its weathered face against the orange
shore, a set of oars left inside.
Do you think the afternoons were longer

as a child because our legs were shorter?
It took more time to cast a fishing line and reel
back. The children ran in the grass and dug
holes in the lawn until we called them home

to wash their faces, unlace their shoes.
I had a pair of red Keds as a girl
when afternoons were outside,
and rain, and boats built in the street.

Beauty Secrets

In plastic lawn chairs next to the lake
we pour olive oil in our hands and run our fingers
through our hair: a beauty secret you'd read quickly
in a grocery line magazine. We take turns wrapping

each other's hair in flowered scarves, tied
at the back. At ten you knew how vitamin E could
cover a face: habit you'd watched your mother
keep before she went to bed. And you joke,

at thirty, that that's why your dad left your mom
when you were twenty and gone to L.A. for sun
and school. It's ok,   I don't know how to say.
But you already know: the lake and trees are big
enough here to keep the secrets that won't leave.

Lantern Bloom

for the girls I mentored in Pomona

Red bougainvillea, a string of paper lanterns
caught fire on your fence,
doesn't end, pressed between the heavy pages
of a book. A girl between fifteen and cutting off
all of her hair tells me that to be an artist necessitates
being happy. She wants to draw better than she does.

East of L.A., smog covers like a single question,
and mountains sit close by. How far does sad
go? she asks. Looking too long can leave eyes
all over the body, until we cry like peacocks,
predicting a day of rain for the hanging vines.

Boxes of Old Photographs

Don't write about what you know; write what will
take your mother's boxes
full of photographs and bobbypins. Questions

are children lifting their hands: why does she wear
stockings to her knees? Why do some men sing
like curtains; why did my mother marry

in a sailor suit? It's how we started asking:
raising our hands into other people's arms.
My father bathed me minutes after I was born

two weeks late. Warm water in a yellow plastic tub.
It was then, my mother tells me, that I was quiet
enough for her to see the eyes we share.

Possums

for J.S.P.

The possums played in our living room: laid
dead-like on the carpet, draped over the rocking
chair, wrapped around lamps. My grandmother

framed pictures of these beady-eyed creatures
and on visits to her house we put together puzzles,
one of a mother, pink-nosed and holding her young

on her back. I never knew they were ugly
or had no choice but teeth until I saw one
crawling limp-step across a half-lit street.

The night had changed them somehow,
the way darkness alters portraits on the walls,
cracked closet doors, and creaks in old houses.

On my dresser sits a glass tree, small as a hand,
where two small possums rest upside down,
tails questioning the window light passing through.

Parking Lot Market

She sells jars of pickled okra, green
and yellow beans, and watermelon rinds.
Her hands, accustomed to pots of vinegar
and garlic, are pruned like a child's toes

too long in a warm bath. Her mother must
have told her stories of jars, myths
of coriander, cilantro, and cinnamon bark,
the only smells that still enchant her.

Snapping beans, she breaks the ends like limbs
and lets the green arms and legs fall to her feet.
There is a worn softness about her skin,
like dirt. If she would only smile, or wink,

children might think to sit cross-legged
in front of her on the hot concrete
and wait for her to tell stories of okra,
of coriander, orange peel, and rind.

Oconee Bells

Its lace requires fine thread,
and white petals that can be pressed
to paper stars between heavy pages
of my parents' *Collier's Encyclopedia*.

Ten years ago two men flew
around the world in a silver balloon,
and the gray whale
was no longer endangered.
Whoever finds this book
in the piles upstairs
might search the name

of these flowers that a book says
were once lost for a hundred years;
and their searching will stitch
the sides of these bells, again.

Curve of the Belly

The woods remind us that a snake sheds
its skin and forges letters on the lake.
Her long body writes the epic differently

out here. Praise the curve of her belly
that makes her body;
and the skin she left
behind. All the weeks of shedding
have led to this: a shore; and what remains

of a delicate history of weeks,
left carefully on the wooden sill
of a porch with rocking chairs.

Moth and Moon

Tonight the moon catches herself unaware
     humming Dvořák, the first music (as we know)
to ever rest in her ears. Moths beside her
     eat stars through the woolen sky. It's dusk

in May and too warm for blankets at the foot
     of our beds, so we sit in rocking chairs
on the porch. The moon finds her reflections
     in the shadows of the lake, while moths
find their way with tiny wings.

They circle our porch light at the foothills
     of the Blue Ridge, away from city haze.
We watch them frenzy their way
     back into the holes we can't fit in
but have looked to for gods since birth.

A History of Hair

Your hair was long for years before we met.
You tell me it used to fall to your knees;
old stories I hear when we lie in bed.

Stars hang from the ceiling above our heads;
paper constellations mapping our sleep:
Your breathing beside me; our hands met;

your hair in a bun at the nape of your neck.
I find it strange that we weren't there to see
the stories we tell each other lying in bed.

I have brown tendrils my mother kept
the first time she cut my hair; a baby
then and years before we had ever met.

Your mother let your locks alone, swept
the floor, and put the wind to work. Tell me
your story when night takes us to bed.

You fall asleep talking, head on my chest;
I kiss the top of your head and recall
how your hair was long years before we met
in stories we told when we lay in bed.

Sun would catch

your hair, have you pulling off your overshirt. All the pictures
on the wall would follow suit, let their edges turn antique,
faces from another era. Birds would fly themselves to paper
and crinkle back again. Our feet wouldn't fall asleep from
    sitting
in one place too long. People would walk in the street, take hats
off their walls to wear outside. A bird can have four thousand
    feathers
open up into a fan, let itself come from that holding place
where a sway is born. The chestnut tree keeps tiny teeth
along the edges of its leaves, would nibble the day
until the air cooled down, and your hair was black again.

III

Calico Street

Dark cannot be measured with hands
the way a room can be marked with feet,
shoe steadily in front of shoe.

The way a fingernail doesn't grow straight
across (but in a sort of moon, matching
the center at its root), the night
will not be kept.

Night is calico there and held high enough
on a linden tree. The shadows of our legs
stop short of road; we have no feet, no leaving
in the night lit with orange lamps and bricks.
Without knowing the extent, I kissed you back
in a tiny room that was barely lit.

After It's Over

Maybe there are not two sides to the story
the way your palm holds your cheek
your life could be summed up in notes
you've scribbled on napkin backs and scraps
of paper in your purse. I've held words
the way grapefruits eat holes in themselves
on the ground next door. I never saw the tree

early enough to know if their insides go
first, if the fruit is already gone when
the hole makes a way to the skin. I learned
to love them first from a girl, in the morning, pink
with a covered sun. She cut its petaled flesh
with a serrated spoon. It's not a simple violence:

this cutting open, down the middle, this taking
to our mouths. After it's all over, we take the rind,
a cup with barely anything left inside, curl
its sides up like a boat and suck what's left
of the juice, a bittersweet, and pulp.

For Julia in Little Armenia

When a rabbit porpoises through snow, a thousand things
      are true at once: you're not close to your father for the
          things
you share: the always being right, the wine, basil that dries
      brown on your windowsill. When I say your name out
          loud:

an inheritance from my grandmother, who saved tap water
      in glass bottles; who kept a jar of broken glass on the
          counter.
But it was soft: glass buried in the ground for years.
      We may have too many things in common: an unlike-
          liness
to hug at first, a quiet in our eyes, a tendency to *miss*
      and *love* too early. When I say your name out loud,
          a mirror
rests on my tongue and turns into a bird when it leaves

my lips. This bird is a strangeness, hearing my own face
      in saying *Julia*. It carries this in its tiny beak,
where a thousand things can be true at once.

Octave

Learning how to live alone: freezing a loaf of bread,
making soup that gets better after days, hanging the mirror
from picture molding with different colors of yarn,
the strings fall unevenly against the wall I painted green.

A young girl practices octaves, rolling her fingers, quiet
over her thighs, while her mother plays piano
for the choir. I wonder if I will keep covering my walls
with pictures, cards I can't quite part with, dried flowers

from my old apartment's street, until my mother's house
is written here. I have learned to hold on from her,
from the refrigerator doors, the stairwell, the nook
turned into a bookcase, full of photographs, drawings
my brother and I gave, the note my dad left on a torn-off
piece of paper on the kitchen table: "love you good"

Early Psalm

Hands tell us what arms
and legs forget: what time has done
to what we've touched.
The mystery of the foreign
in the fog
burned off early
in the mid-summer sun,
found us warm in bed. My wrist
left open to the palm
taken in yours. Lives read
by the lines
that nights intersect.

Buttered Toast

Someone who takes signs from the flight of birds
says dreaming of toast is an auspicious omen.
Quietly, before she takes the morning bus to work,

I tell her she painted our claw-foot tub red, curled
inside the tusk of an elephant, sang and sewed
our buttons back. From high up there, a bird

carried her letters, telling me he charged faster
than water ran. I buttered toast and closed
it back inside the bird's beak. Late to work,

she tells me to write the rest down, save her
dried dirt on the elephant's back, how cold
she wrote the inside of a tooth could be. Birds

take the crumbs of toast I toss for squirrels,
but that night we take our dinner outside and hope
we'll see one attempt to shimmy, hard at work

up the slippery red pole of the birdhouse, search
brave, upside-down for seeds. By then, I've forgotten
the gray smell of elephant; the flight of that bird,
and draw a bath, ivory tooth to hold her after work.

Plaster Dust

Not everyone holds their dreams, but my brother
remembers being three years old, kneeing through

plaster dust when the upstairs was being carved out
of the attic. I would have been five, and dreamed last

night that he covered my face, one small hand
over each of my eyes. I wasn't five, though,

like you'd think. Being older didn't make sense
when I opened my eyes. But, dreams are gods

who make seas in an afternoon, a million species
of laughter in an hour, the kind of vine that spills

onto a street in minutes, up a freeway wall, across
a chicken fence, the length of a lover's name. Dreams
need room, a forgotten place to remember us with.

Hold Like Owls

You wear your hair like curtains, drawn down
to sigh, a word you could go on without
translating, breath the throat can't own

and chest won't keep. Your eyes hold like owls,
but they're blue: the difference
between the bird and girl. Rocks drawn down

a mountain leave shadows of your face, found
centuries before. It's too dark to tell if pink
held your cheeks even then. Throat can't own

what's in the air. The sky's as tired as you are now
and have been before. Why do you think the river
holds so many stones? Wear your hair down

your shoulder. The air singing clings to, mouths
won't bottle for tiny ships. No, the birds still
wander without translating arias of their own.

Wings look effortless. Try singing out loud
and mouth the words that won't come, until
you wear your hair like curtains, drawn down
to curl against your cheeks, a score of its own.

Even Haystacks

We must learn to laugh at ourselves. To gather
into our bellies and shake loose in the snow.
We sled on our stomachs down a road blocked off
for the season; a mountain path too steep to plow.

Here, even haystacks get covered with winter
and dogs grow beards in the snow. We eat
dinner with the oven open, the car packed
into the driveway all day with no where to go.

One Afternoon

You tell me kissing
is more
intimate than sex

as if your parted
lips cradle
some part of you

that can still be
taken. It is there
in the parting

that you are
as unconcerned as glass
about its breaking.

Yet it is the possibility
of shatter where
glass is glass
at all.

My Quixote

for C.J.S.

All that you need to know of a man are the lines
that make him: the sun is a circle; the sword
is a straight line; the horizon, broken; the wind,
in between. I watch him twist the thin string

of a teabag around his finger with the rugged
gentleness of horses or a beard. He rests
his cup on his wearing jeans and tells me the trees
that line the highway fields turned red as a girl's

hair: impractical as all things that fall. I wrap
both hands around my warm mug until they meet
and move closer to him on the back steps.

Losing Noon

Some days I stay in bed past noon to find
I cannot get back
to where the scent

of your hair is all
that falls between us. And the space
is slow as dreams are, even falling

from a tree climbed as a girl, not knowing,
still, what it is to land on feet. Sleep slows
love down like dying. And I realize that life

must not flash before us in death; it moves us
slowly through what we cannot get back,
and as in sleep, our eyes need not be open.

When It Starts to Rain in San Francisco

We walk into a stripclub at noon
and the only other person
there is a man on lunch break.

He might work for those damp
dollars he gives the girls
that look him in the eye.

But we're there, too,
buying the house vodka
and trying not to

look awkwardly from their breasts
to their high heels to each other,
thinking how worldly we are to sit
with a city on a Tuesday afternoon.

IV

As Far as March

One must have a mind of spring:
to have been warm a long time; to have watched
the azaleas turn pink along the drive; to learn to love
the wind again; to wait for the tadpoles to leave the algaed
edges of the pond and grow legs; to fall asleep with windows
open; to sit cross-legged in the grass and tie flowers
together by their stems; to forget that what blossoms
will again waste away.

Hidden There

We were only eight then
hiding notes in that small box
made of cardboard, with leaves
glued to its top and sides to disguise
its place in a large azalea bush
halfway between our two houses.

To reach the box, we had to put our hands
through branches of leaves and pink
where bees hid, unaware of their hiding,
taking what they needed from the flowers
and leaving part of what they came with.

Joy, the Elephant, Greenville Zoo, 1990

Her cage was the one at the top of the hill: pool
dirty with upcountry clay, two tires scattered
in dust, a few blocks of hay to keep the ground
from running when it rained. Thick-skinned

and dry, beast which Aristotle wrote
passeth all others in wit and mind, accompanied
the lonely river my grandmother walked
with my brother and me some Saturdays.

She danced by herself in the rise and fall
of a one-two-three, the drag of her feet, her heavy
trunk and tusks in the afternoon. In the mail years
later, my grandmother wrote that Joy had died:

a newspaper photograph showed her gait,
her widening eyes. She looked quite weightless,
as I remember, a sort of waltz in her thighs.

Counting Pelicans

Marsh grasses weave through the holes
      minnows swim through in her lace skirt.
She had lived near the river that turned

into an estuary where pelicans flew in long rows.
      After breakfast and sometimes in late afternoon,
she had put herself to sleep by counting. Focused

on the way the birds hit the water and came back
      to the surface. They had looked so awkwardly graceful
when they took the fish, held them in great beaks,
      cradled into another place.

Encounters with Buzzards

Perched on top of an interstate streetlight
one buzzard holds his head high over five-o'clock
traffic. No older than nine, she'd held a bike

close to her chest at the back of that small,
white church left on afternoons.
That's where she saw him, with the dead,
taking what we always left to disappear

on the side of highways. That one afternoon
taught her to distrust the backside of churches
where grass grew in tufts next to stones, slowly
losing the names carved on their faces.

There were no prayers hunched under his back.
Only the necessity of scavage and the shining
black feathers leathering his neck.

December Hemlock

The trees are safe in the cold, white sort
        of grieving covering a field; ground only
flawed at the edge of the road
        where cars turn white to mud.

She counts the hemlock rings at the trunk
        where beavers cut back
through years. The ponds have turned
        to spilled milk, but no one would hear
her crying out here in the woods, quiet with snow.

Blue House on Wheat Street

A hundred years of plaster and glass forget
slowly what to hold and what not to let slip
through its cracks. The walls moved like trees

on certain days in spring, but she loved the light
that came unabashedly from its windows left
uncurtained after noon. She grew older

on days she stayed inside listening to leaves
blanketing the roof. Growing older, she thought,
meant finally letting herself be chipped away,
white paint revealing a bright layer of blue.

Larks at Dawn

You know better with wings than we can
      with arms and legs. You are closer to where
air is no longer air, where stars are held

and the moon begins. Yes, you are held up there
      like that, escaping, for a time, the drag
of dirt and sin. We set our homes on fire when wind
      can do nothing but catch. Branches singed
and black, early with the morning lights.

Kume and the Washerwoman

after the Japanese legend

i. Fallen

What makes us love what we cannot hold,
that which draws us to fall into the water
where women wash their dirty clothes?

Wasn't I a god before I saw her, bold
and robed in clouds? I knew the thoughts
that make mortals love what they cannot hold:

A pattern of wanting what's forbidden,
fruit and places touched that must be bought
with blame and cleaned like dirty clothes.

They say it was her thigh where I lost my hold
on everything above, the knowing that knew her,
distanced as sun from the grey of winter's hold.

But it was her dark eyes that found me, showed
me what it was to be born out of water,
the river where women wash their clothes.

Loving her meant knowing what was old;
for time became something that mattered.
And what makes fools love what they cannot hold,
I found in that woman washing clothes.

ii. *Worn Too Thin*

Don't all ideals of love fade with the passing fish?
Silvered scales move down rivers bedded in stone,
and what we think is love too soon wears thin.

Love is better to look at from above, I told him.
There, my hair will never be unspun from gold.
Here, ideals of love only fade with the passing fish.

The cherry blossoms quickly leave barren limbs.
Everyone wants to fall in love in the spring, born
anew with the leaves, but those, too, wear thin.

Branches left with just a black bird's kiss.
Your waning from the sky will leave you alone,
for what you think is love will soon wear you thin.

But you became a mortal and fell into the river.
You came to me on the back of a carp, slow
and bearing yellows and reds faded from fish.

I knew love in the touch of your painted skin
bruised by rocks at the river's bottom. With you,
ideals of love may return with the passing fish,
and our questioning will never wear us too thin.

Painting on Silk

after "The Ghost of Oyuki"

Art bares the beauty that we cannot speak,
so I paint what I remember to forget,

the way you brushed your face white, careful
with the curved lines, nape of your neck.

To paint is to know layers up close,
brushstrokes of brown that shadow

your brow; curve of your lips, down.
I stand back to make sense of the lines there

on silk, to understand your body
from a distance never practiced before.

Ruin

for A.M.W.S.

Praise the wind heavy with frying onion and dust
        that covers us in the streets of Athens. I had thought

I was a fool to think this place could save us.
        Place apart, where art is old. But the two of us sitting

on this cold marble floor in a broken-down
        church find something in the faded Byzantine

scenes on its walls. Hands and breath have changed
        the paint, reds gone to orange with age and praise.

CPSIA information can be obtained at www.ICGtesting.com
Printed in the USA
LVOW042148150412

277684LV00006B/4/P